I Am Malala

Lightbox Literature Studies

Michelle Lomberg and Katie Gillespie

LIGHTBOX
openlightbox.com

LIGHTBOX

Go to
www.openlightbox.com
and enter this book's
unique code.

ACCESS CODE

LBXC6429

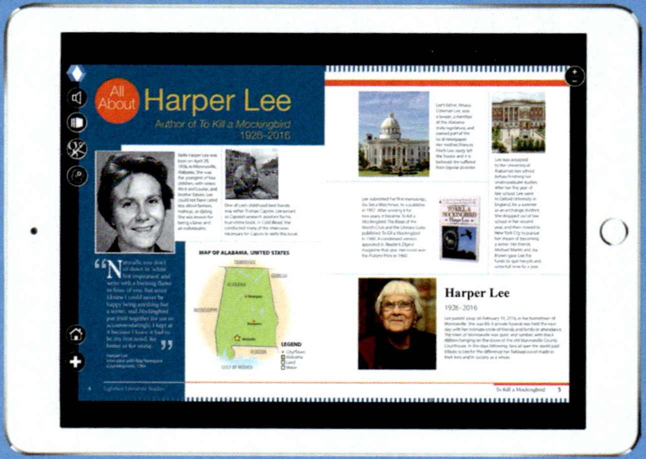

Lightbox is an all-inclusive digital solution for the teaching and learning of curriculum topics in an original, groundbreaking way. Lightbox is based on National Curriculum Standards.

STANDARD FEATURES OF LIGHTBOX

AUDIO High-quality narration using text-to-speech system

VIDEOS Embedded high-definition video clips

ACTIVITIES Printable PDFs that can be emailed and graded

WEBLINKS Curated links to external, child-safe resources

SLIDESHOWS Pictorial overviews of key concepts

TRANSPARENCIES Step-by-step layering of maps, diagrams, charts, and timelines

INTERACTIVE MAPS Interactive maps and aerial satellite imagery

QUIZZES Ten multiple choice questions that are automatically graded and emailed for teacher assessment

KEY WORDS Matching key concepts to their definitions

MORE Extra information and details on the subject

FIRST HAND Letters, diaries, and other primary sources

DOCS Speeches, newspaper articles, and other historical documents

Contents

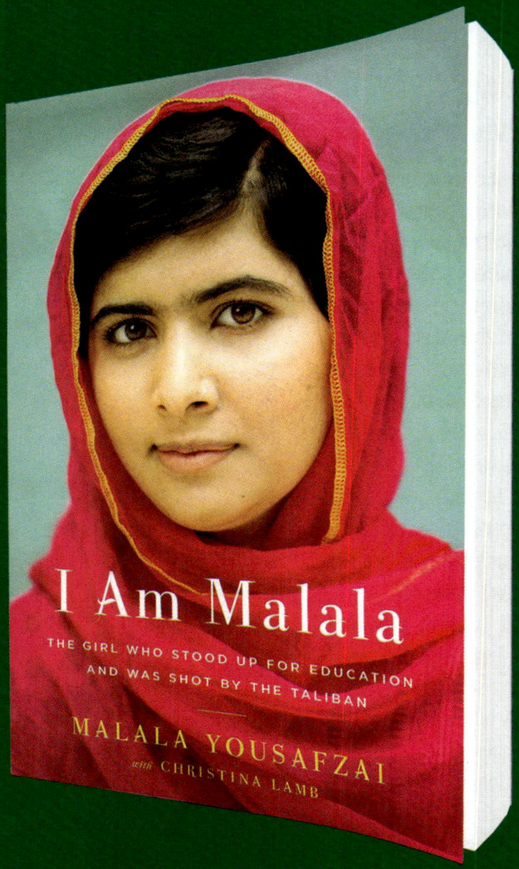
I Am Malala
THE GIRL WHO STOOD UP FOR EDUCATION AND WAS SHOT BY THE TALIBAN
MALALA YOUSAFZAI
with CHRISTINA LAMB

RUBRIC

Conducting an Interview

Students will conduct an interview with a community member about a time period in their community's history, and submit an audio recording and transcript of the interview. An exemplary interview will meet the following criteria.

- Clearly defines the purpose of the interview
- Conducts thorough background research to inform the focus of the interview and the questions
- Drafts a complete list of thoughtful, in-depth, and varied questions prior to the interview
- Interviews a subject with relevant knowledge on the topic and time period in question
- Asks questions in a logical order, building upon each other
- Treats the interview subject in a polite, respectful, and professional manner
- Does not interrupt or rush the interview subject
- Shows interest and enthusiasm in responses and follow-up questions
- Chooses follow-up questions that demonstrate active listening
- Asks for clarification and further details when necessary
- Asks questions about personal experiences related to the topic
- Asks questions regarding factual information and the interview subject's opinion on the topic
- Asks creative questions that reflect fresh insights on the topic
- Records the full interview in a quiet environment
- Organizes and edits the interview transcript to be clear and factual

All About Malala Yousafzai

1997–

Known around the world as the girl who was shot in the head by the **Taliban**, Malala Yousafzai is an **activist** who campaigns for the right of all children to receive an education. Malala was born on July 12, 1997, in Mingora, Pakistan. She has two younger brothers. Khushal was born in 1999, and Atal was born five years later. Malala's mother, Toor Pekai Yousafzai, is a pious woman. Illiterate for most of her life , she began learning to read and write in 2012, when Malala was 15. Despite not having an education herself, Toor Pekai supports her children's academic efforts. Malala's father, Ziauddin Yousafzai, is an educator and activist. He came from a large family, with one brother and five sisters. His father, Rohul Amin, was a high school theology teacher, an **imam**, and a respected public speaker.

> "I began to see that the pen and the words that come from it can be much more powerful than machine guns, tanks or helicopters. We were learning how to struggle. And we were learning how powerful we are when we speak."
>
> Malala Yousafzai,
> Chapter 13: The Diary of Gul Makai

MAP OF THE UNITED KINGDOM AND PAKISTAN

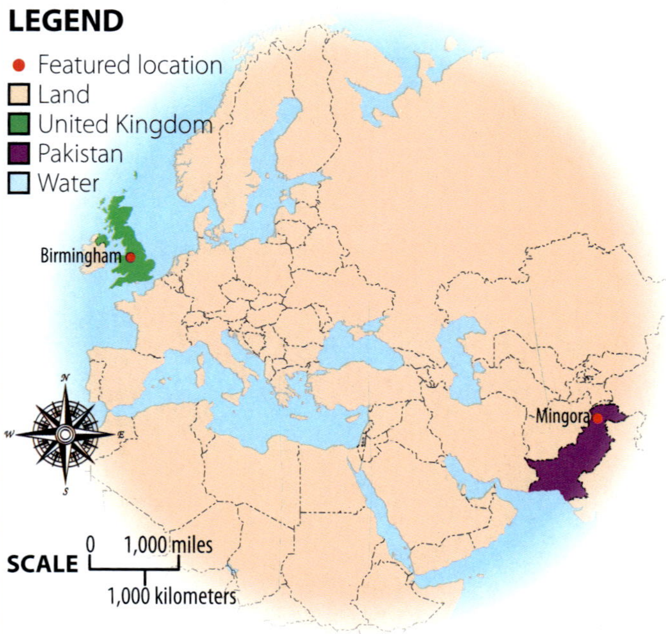

Malala grew up in Mingora, in Pakistan's Swat district. Toor Pekai was a stay-at-home mother who cared for Malala and her brothers. Ziauddin was a founder of Khushal School in Mingora. Long before she was old enough to attend, Malala had the run of the school and was a favorite of the teachers. In January 2009, the Taliban, who were powerful in Swat, closed schools for girls. In May 2009, war forced the Yousafzais to leave the Swat Valley. The Pakistani army was attempting to drive out the Taliban, and the resulting turmoil made it unsafe to remain in the area. The family settled in Karshat, Toor Pekai's village, and Malala attended school with her cousin. Khushal School reopened in August.

As the Taliban gained influence in the Swat Valley, it opposed education for girls with increasing violence. Following in her father's footsteps, Malala became an outspoken activist for the right of girls to attend school. In 2009, she began a blog written under the pseudonym Gul Makai. The blog was posted on the BBC News Urdu website. It described life under Taliban rule, and was read by people around the world. Malala and her father gave talks and television interviews in Pakistan, and *The New York Times* featured a video documentary about her. Today, Malala continues to **advocate** for the right of all children to attend school through the Malala Fund.

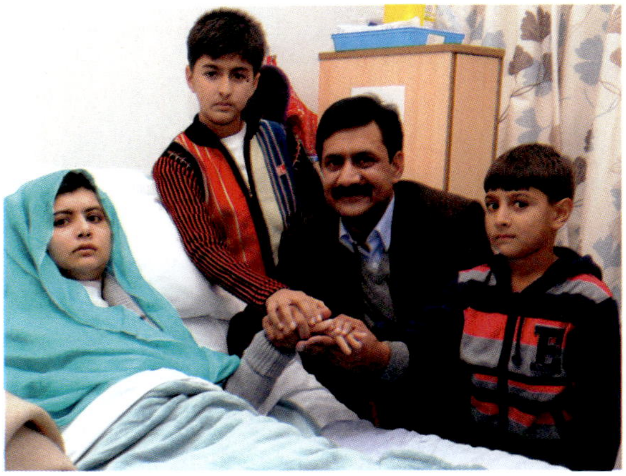

Malala's opposition to the Taliban almost cost the young girl her life. On October 9, 2012, a Taliban gunman boarded Malala's school bus, shooting her and two other girls. A bullet entered Malala's head above her left eye and came to rest near her left shoulder blade. She was initially treated in Pakistan, but her care team believed she would receive the best rehabilitation in the United Kingdom, so she was flown to Birmingham. Malala's family reunited with her in Birmingham 10 days later. She was discharged from hospital in January 2013. The Yousafzai family continues to live in Birmingham, while Malala began studies in philosophy, politics, and economics at Oxford University in 2017.

ACTIVITIES

Google Maps

Mingora, Pakistan

Explore Malala's hometown of Mingora, Pakistan, using street view.

First Hand

Our Q&A with Malala Yousafzai, Nobel Peace Prize winner and education advocate

Examine this Lily News interview with Malala by Petra Eriksson.

1. What types of questions does the interviewer ask? What topics does she focus on? Why would she focus on these specific areas?
2. In the interview, Malala says that her parents are her role models. She claims that "My parents didn't think I was less than my brothers because I'm a girl." How is this attitude a departure from traditional cultural views? Why is this significant?

RUBRIC

Researching for a Writing Assignment

Students will complete a thorough research process to prepare for a writing assignment, and organize their research in a logical manner that supports their writing. An exemplary research process will meet the following criteria.

- Creates a goal for the research, based on the topic and working thesis
- Creates specific, thoughtful, and inventive research questions that are relevant to the topic of the writing assignment
- Produces a list of categories, key words, and related ideas to effectively assist in researching
- Uses high-quality sources that pertain to the topic and come in a variety of formats, such as books, journals, primary sources, websites, and databases
- Determines accuracy of all sources
- Uses sources that provide balanced research and various perspectives on the topic in question
- Takes notes to highlight the key facts and ideas in order to answer all research questions
- Extracts relevant, detailed information from the sources during the note-taking process
- Organizes the research notes in a clear and concise manner
- Organizes the research notes logically and in a way that sets up the information and ideas for analysis and the writing process
- Analyzes the information and produces ideas and points to support the working thesis
- Uses an effective and suitable format to present all research
- Properly cites all sources used

Setting of the Memoir

Snapshot

Falak Sar, Swat's highest peak, is **19, 416 feet tall**. (5,918 meters)

In 2017, the population of **Mingora, Pakistan** was **279,914**.

There are **6,123 Pashto speakers** in Birmingham.

It takes approximately **7 hours** and **49 minutes** to travel by plane from **Islamabad**, Pakistan to **London**, England.

Most of *I Am Malala* takes place in Pakistan's Swat Valley. The Republic of Pakistan is a country in South Asia. It is bordered by Afghanistan and Iran on the west, China in the north, India on the east, and the Arabian Sea on the south. With a total area of 307,374 square miles (796,095 square kilometers), Pakistan is the thirty-sixth largest country in the world. Geographically, its landmass can be divided into three regions. These are the northern highlands, the Indus River plain, and the Balochistan Plateau. The climate includes desert, temperate, and arctic zones. Pakistan's mountain ranges include the Hindu Kush and the western Himalayas. The country has 650 miles (1,046 km) of coastline. The Indus is Pakistan's most important river, supplying most of the country's household and agricultural water.

A young country, Pakistan was created as a homeland for India's Muslims when Great Britain granted India independence from colonial rule in 1947. Pakistan remains a Muslim country, with more than 96 percent of the population practicing Islam, the official religion. Today, Pakistan's population is more than 200 million, making it the sixth most populous country on Earth. Punjabis are the largest ethnic group in Pakistan, followed by Pashtuns, the group to which Malala and her family belong. Urdu, one of the country's two official languages along with English, is spoken by 8 percent of the population. Pashto, the language of the Pashtun people, is spoken by 15 percent of the population.

Swat Valley

"We lived in the most beautiful place in all the world. My valley, the Swat Valley, is a heavenly kingdom of mountains, gushing waterfalls and crystal-clear lakes. WELCOME TO PARADISE, it says on a sign as you enter the valley."

Malala Yousafzai, Chapter 1: A Daughter Is Born

Swat is part of Khyber Pakhtunkhwa province in northwest Pakistan. Known as the Switzerland of the East, this mountainous region has a temperate climate that allows orchards to flourish, and boasts Pakistan's first ski resort. Swat has a rich history. The region was once a Buddhist kingdom, and ruins of ancient temples and statues of Buddha are still found there. Malala's hometown of Mingora is the region's largest city. Malala lived in a flat-roofed house in the neighborhood of Gulkada.

Malala's parents grew up in villages in the remote and mountainous Shangla district. The Yousafzais return to Shangla to celebrate the Eid holidays twice a year. The family fled to Shangla when fighting forced them from Mingora in 2009.

The Yousafzai House

"Our house feels big and empty. It sits behind an electric iron gate and it sometimes seems as if we are in what we in Pakistan call a sub-jail, a kind of luxury house arrest. At the back there is a large garden with lots of trees for me and my brothers to play cricket in. But there are no rooftops to play on, no children fighting with kites in the streets, no neighbors coming in to borrow a plate of rice or for us to ask for three tomatoes."

Malala Yousafzai, Epilogue: One Child, One Teacher, One Book, One Pen...

Following her gunshot wound, Malala was treated in both Peshawar and Rawalpindi, then transferred to the Queen Elizabeth Hospital in Birmingham, where she and her family eventually settled. Birmingham is situated roughly 110 miles (177 km) northwest of London in the West Midlands. It is the second-largest city in the United Kingdom. Founded in the Middle Ages, Birmingham rose to prominence during the **Industrial Revolution**, and it remains an important industrial center.

ACTIVITIES

Video

Class Dismissed in Swat Valley - Malala Yousafzai News | The New York Times

Discover more about Malala and the closure of her school by the Taliban by watching this 2009 video by *The New York Times*.

1. At the time this video was filmed, it was decided that the Yousafzais would not leave the Swat Valley. How might Malala's story be different if her family had not been forced to leave Pakistan?
2. The setting of Malala's story comes from her own real-life experiences. How do you think the memoir would be different if it were written somewhere else?

Weblink

Malala Yousafzai on life in Britain: 'We have never seen women so free'

Learn more about Malala's experience of settling into her new life in Birmingham, England.

1. In the article, Malala says that the adjustment to life in England was particularly difficult for her mother "because we have never seen that women would be that much free." How is this different from the lives of women in Pakistan? What are the positive and negative effects of such a dramatic life change? Why?
2. Malala clearly states that she is "not becoming western." Why is it important for her to continue following her culture? How is this reflected in *I Am Malala*?

Time Period of the Memoir

I Am Malala spans the 15 years between Malala's birth in 1997 and her move to England following her gunshot wound in 2012. This period coincides with incidents of violent upheaval in Pakistan and around the world, including the attack on Malala and her classmates.

Pakistan in the Twenty-first Century

The first decade of the twenty-first century was a time of upheaval in Pakistan, including Malala's beloved Swat Valley. Although Pakistan was not involved in the September 11, 2001, attacks on the World Trade Center in New York City, the resulting bombing of neighboring Afghanistan by American forces destabilized the region. Americans pursued Afghanistan-based **terrorists** into Pakistan, launching the first **drone** strikes in 2004. Osama bin Laden, the instigator of the 9/11 attack, fled to Pakistan, where he was killed in 2011.

Between 2005 and 2009, Swat was under the influence of the Taliban. Local Taliban leader Maulana Fazlullah launched his radio station in 2005. He used this medium to preach Islamic **extremism**. That same year, Pakistan was struck by an earthquake that killed more than 70,000 people. As a result of the Taliban's rescue and relief efforts, they were able to consolidate their influence in the area. By 2007, Fazlullah was setting up Islamic courts in the region.

In 2007, Benazir Bhutto, a former prime minister of Pakistan, returned from abroad to run in the country's elections. She was a role model for girls such as Malala, and a symbol of hope for all who valued **democracy** and wanted to end extremism. On the day she arrived in Karachi, Bhutto survived an **assassination** attempt in which **militants** blew up her bus. In December that year, another attack claimed her life.

Attacks on Pakistan

"Militants had killed Benazir, blown up the country's best-known hotel, killed thousands of people in suicide bombings and beheadings and destroyed hundreds of schools. What more would it take for the army and government to resist them?"

Malala Yousafzai, Chapter 14: A Funny Kind of Peace

Following Benazir Bhutto's assassination, the Taliban continued to gain strength. In 2009, an estimated 2 to 3.5 million people, including the Yousafzais, became **internally displaced persons** as a result of conflict between the Taliban and the Pakistani army.

Malala's School Closes

"When I got home, I cried and cried. I didn't want to stop learning. I was only eleven years old, but felt as though I had lost everything. I had told everyone in my class that the Taliban wouldn't go through with it. 'They're just like our politicians—they talk the talk, but they won't do anything,' I'd said. But then they went ahead and closed our school and I felt embarrassed."

Malala Yousafzai, Chapter 13: The Diary of Gul Makai

ACTIVITIES

First Hand

Diary of a Pakistani schoolgirl
Discover more about Malala by reading her BBC News blog.

1. Choose one of the blog entries for further reflection. What is the tone of the entry? How does Malala use language to connect with readers? Why do you think it was necessary for Malala to use a pseudonym when writing the blog?
2. How did the time period that *I Am Malala* was written in impact Malala's creation of the memoir? In what ways might the story be different if it were written today?

Weblink

Interactive Timeline: Malala Yousafzai's Extraordinary Journey
Examine the timeline to learn more about the events of Malala's story.

1. What were the impacts of the 2009 ceasefire collapse on the Swat Valley? How were Malala and her family affected? How are these events portrayed in the memoir?
2. When did Malala first receive global recognition? How do you think she dealt with her newfound fame? Explain your answer by citing evidence from the memoir.

RUBRIC

Writing a Short Story

Students will choose an excerpt from the memoir and use it as their inspiration in writing a short story. An exemplary short story will meet the following criteria.

- Engages the reader from the opening line
- Establishes a clear, consistent point of view
- Introduces a narrator and a setting
- Develops an engaging conflict at the heart of the narrative to build tension and keep the reader interested
- Develops characters and events through purposeful and well-crafted literary devices
- Creates a logical progression of events in the narrative that build upon each other using various techniques
- Explores ideas, concepts, and writing styles with creativity and originality
- Demonstrates a high level of skill in using appropriate narrative techniques to tell the story
- Concludes the narrative in a thoughtful, effective manner appropriate to the narrative
- Uses varied, purposeful diction and syntax to affect style and serve the narrative
- Writes with clarity, imagination, and a unique, personal voice
- Does not use stereotypes or clichés
- Uses effective, believable dialogue
- Uses correct spelling, grammar, and punctuation

Conflict in the Memoir

Every story has a conflict, even a non-fiction story such as a memoir. Conflict occurs when the main character, or protagonist, faces obstacles in reaching his or her goals. These obstacles may be external or they may come from within. A story can have more than one kind of conflict.

The Four Major Types of Conflict in Literature

In a man versus man conflict, the protagonist is pitted against an antagonist. This character tries to prevent the protagonist from reaching a goal, and may even threaten the protagonist's life. In Richard Connell's *The Most Dangerous Game*, the protagonist, Rainsford, finds himself on the island of General Zaroff. There, he must fight for his life when the general hunts him down like an animal.

A man versus man conflict takes place between the main character and his or her own feelings or beliefs. In Edgar Allan Poe's *The Tell-Tale Heart*, the narrator kills a man and is driven mad by his own guilty conscience. Believing that the heartbeat of his victim is audible to the police who are questioning him, he confesses to the crime.

In a man versus society conflict, the main character is in conflict with the norms or prejudices in his or her society. In *1984*, George Orwell portrays an intrusive, authoritarian society. Winston, the protagonist, struggles against this society's strictly enforced rules in his quest for freedom and love.

In a man versus nature conflict, the main character is in a battle against the forces of nature, which may take the form of a hostile landscape, climate, animal, or natural disaster. In Herman Melville's *Moby Dick*, Ahab, who has lost his leg to a great white whale, pursues the creature with single-minded obsession.

Types of Conflict in *I Am Malala*

In *I Am Malala*, the protagonist and others find themselves in conflict with society, each other, and nature. Malala was born into a culture in which boys are valued more highly than girls. In fact, when she was born, nobody congratulated her parents. The citizens of Swat were also plagued with natural disasters, such as a flood in 2010.

Man versus Society

"I am very proud to be Pashtun, but sometimes I think our **code of conduct** has a lot to answer for, particularly where the treatment of women is concerned. A woman named Shahida who worked for us and had three small daughters told me that when she was only ten years old her father had sold her to an old man who already had a wife but wanted a younger one. When girls disappeared it was not always because they had been married off."

I Am Malala, "The Village"

Man versus Man

"'Let's get back to the subject of the school,' said the mufti, who could see the discussion was not going his way. 'There are men in the reception area of the school, and they see the girls enter, and this is very bad.'

'I have a solution,' said my father. 'The school has another gate. The girls will enter through that.'

The mufti clearly wasn't happy, as he wanted the school closed altogether. But the elders were happy with this compromise and they left."

I Am Malala, "The Mufti Who Tried to Close Our School"

Man versus Nature

"People had desperately tried to protect what little they owned, moving their animals to higher ground, but the floods saturated the corn they had harvested, destroyed the orchards and drowned many of the buffaloes. The villagers were helpless. They had no power, as all their makeshift hydroelectric projects had been smashed to pieces. They had no clean water, as the river was brown with wreckage and debris."

I Am Malala, "The Valley of Sorrows"

ACTIVITIES

More

The Types of Conflict in *I Am Malala*

Analyze the excerpts from the memoir revealing the types of conflict as they appear in *I Am Malala*.

1. How do these excerpts of conflict reveal the memoir's theme? How do they reveal character? Explain and defend your ideas.
2. Write an analysis of Malala's development of conflict between Malala and the Taliban. What deeper truths may be suggested about these characters as a result of their conflict?

Video

Conflict in Literature

Explore the four different kinds of literary conflicts in this video.

1. Explain each of the four types of conflicts in your own words. Provide examples of each. They can be from plays, novels, short stories, films, or television shows.
2. What is the difference between an internal conflict and an external conflict? Can you think of any similarities between them?

Introducing the Characters

In fiction and non-fiction, readers learn about characters by paying attention to what they say, what they do, and what others say about them. Sometimes, authors describe characters directly, giving their own or the narrator's point of view. Other times, authors present characters indirectly by showing the reader their words and actions, leaving the reader to draw conclusions.

Major Characters in *I Am Malala*

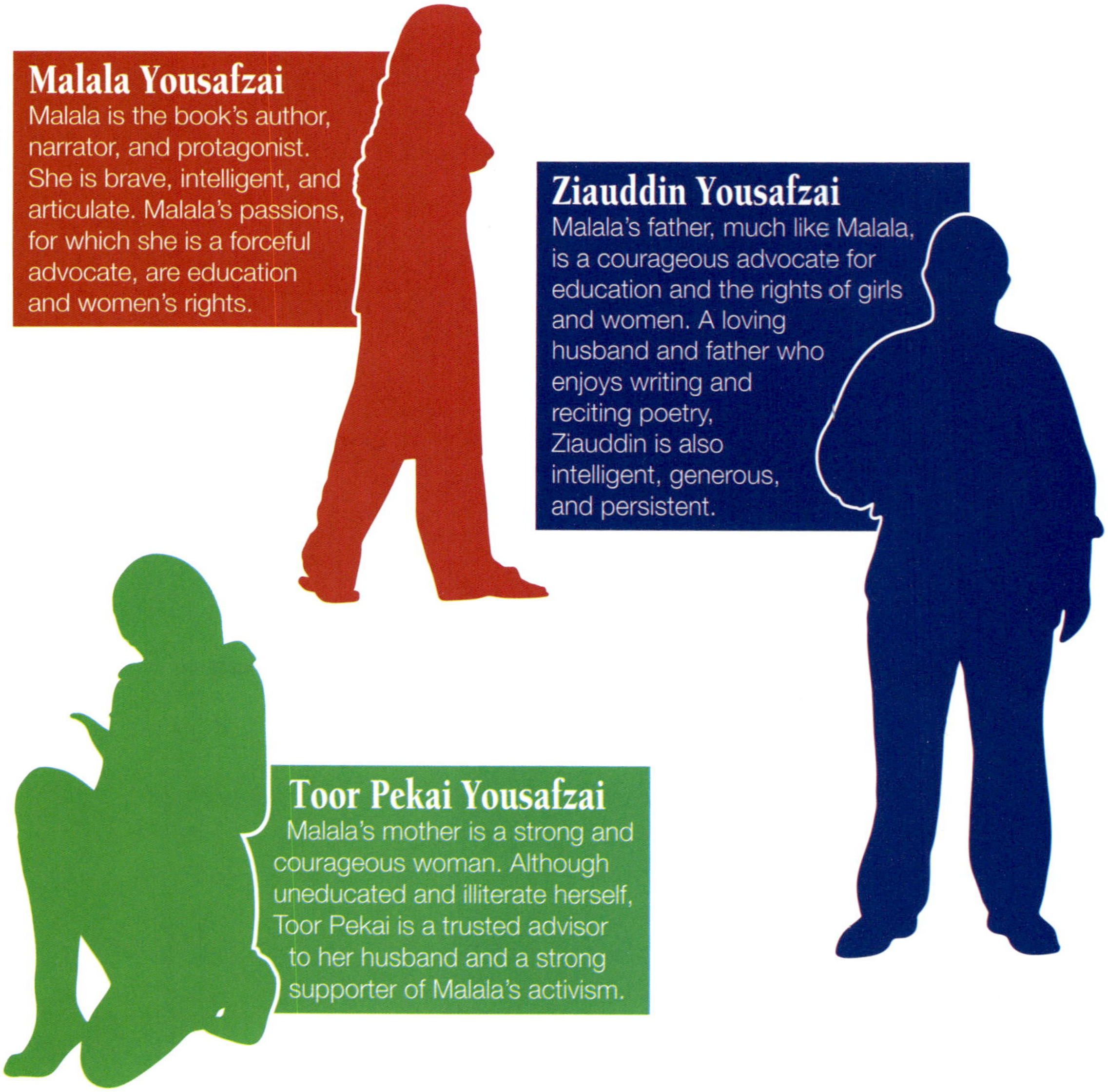

Malala Yousafzai
Malala is the book's author, narrator, and protagonist. She is brave, intelligent, and articulate. Malala's passions, for which she is a forceful advocate, are education and women's rights.

Ziauddin Yousafzai
Malala's father, much like Malala, is a courageous advocate for education and the rights of girls and women. A loving husband and father who enjoys writing and reciting poetry, Ziauddin is also intelligent, generous, and persistent.

Toor Pekai Yousafzai
Malala's mother is a strong and courageous woman. Although uneducated and illiterate herself, Toor Pekai is a trusted advisor to her husband and a strong supporter of Malala's activism.

Malala shows readers the people around her both directly and indirectly. She offers her candid opinions about them, and reports their actions, speech, and what others say about them. Since readers see the characters only from Malala's point of view, they do not have access to the characters' own unspoken thoughts and emotions, as they might in a work of fiction.

Static characters remain unchanged over the course of a story, while dynamic characters change as a result of the story's events. Round characters are complex, with multiple and often contradictory traits. Flat characters reveal only one distinguishing trait. The protagonist is almost always a dynamic, round character.

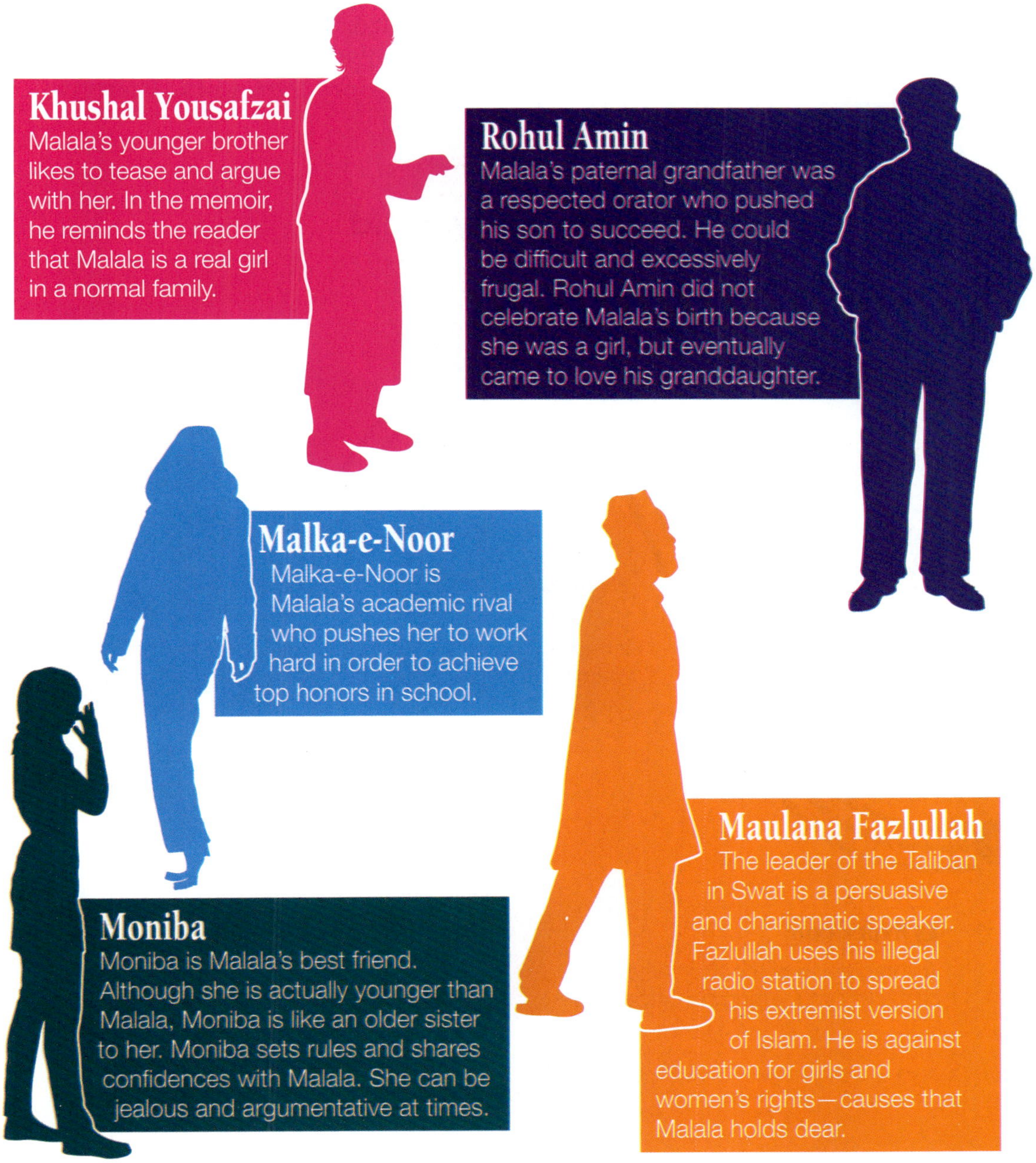

ACTIVITIES

Document

PERSONALITY OF MALALA REFLECTED IN MALALA YOUSAFZAI & CHRISTINA LAMB'S I AM MALALA (2013) MEMOIR: A PSYCHOANALYTIC APPROACH

Review the article by Caecilia Tiewuk Novyanti about Malala's personality, as reflected in *I Am Malala*.

1. Who do you think is the intended audience for this document? Why? Are the tone and language used appropriate for this audience? Explain your answer.
2. What are the main points of the document and how are they presented? Are these points conveyed effectively to the reader? Why or why not?

More

Character Development in *I Am Malala*

Analyze the characters in *I Am Malala* using the descriptions on the character map and excerpts from each character. Then, choose a character and answer the following questions.

1. Which of the writer's techniques are most effective at revealing this character's traits? Why?
2. In what ways is the characterization of this character ineffective? What could be done to improve this character's function in the memoir? Defend your ideas with evidence.

RUBRIC

Creating a Literary Device Analysis Booklet

Students will analyze the author's use of a literary device in the memoir, and create a booklet to present this analysis. An exemplary literary device analysis booklet will meet the following criteria.

- Defines the chosen literary device accurately and in detail
- Places the definition of the literary device at the beginning of the booklet
- Provides strong, specific examples of how this literary device is used in the memoir
- Describes examples in detail, with quotations properly integrated
- Includes thorough analysis of the use, purpose, and effectiveness of each example of how the chosen literary device is used in the memoir
- Arranges all pages logically
- Examples are organized chronologically
- Provides no more than one example and its analysis per page
- Creates a neat, well-organized, and attractive booklet
- Booklet is colorful and displays the student's creativity
- Uses illustrations to represent the chosen literary device and the examples of how it is used in the memoir

The Art of Storytelling

Storytelling is an ancient art that can take many forms. Writers such as Malala have at their disposal many literary devices with which to craft their narratives. In her memoir, Malala uses a number of literary devices to persuade, paint scenes, and convey emotion.

Structure of a Narrative

Regardless of the genre, all stories need to be organized into a coherent structure. One common model of such a structure is Freytag's Pyramid. In this model, events in the plot are aligned along a five-stage, pyramid-shaped framework. These five components are all present in *I Am Malala.*

Freytag's Pyramid

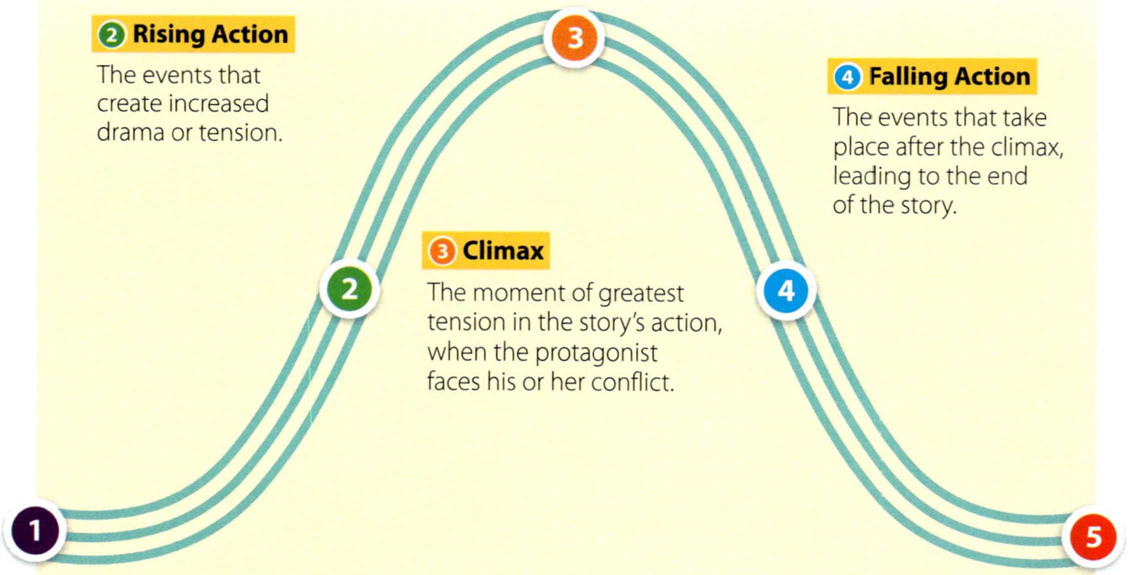

2 Rising Action
The events that create increased drama or tension.

4 Falling Action
The events that take place after the climax, leading to the end of the story.

3 Climax
The moment of greatest tension in the story's action, when the protagonist faces his or her conflict.

1 Exposition
The beginning of the story, where the characters and setting are introduced.

5 Resolution
The end of the story, when the conflicts are resolved and the action comes to a conclusion.

Plot

Every story has a plot, or sequence of events with a beginning, a middle, and an end. Events in the plotline—the order in which events take place in time—must follow each other in a logical sequence. An author may tell a story out of order, beginning in the middle and using flashback and flash-forward techniques.

Plot Points in the Prologue of *I Am Malala*

1. Malala arrives at school.
2. Malala and her classmates say their morning prayers and continue with their school day.
3. Malala's school day ends, and she boards the bus home.
4. The bus begins its route, passing an army checkpoint.
5. The bus is stopped by a young man asking for information about some students.
6. Another young man boards the bus, asking, "Who is Malala?"
7. The man draws a handgun and fires three shots, injuring three girls.
8. The bus arrives at the hospital.

Literary Devices

A literary device is any feature of literature that can be identified, studied, and analyzed. There are two types of literary devices. These are literary elements and literary techniques.

Literary Elements

Literary elements can be used to build meaning, intrigue, suspense, and feeling. Authors use literary elements to create a connection between readers and their story.

Foil

A foil is a character whose traits contrast with and draw attention to those of another character.

Point of View

Point of view is the perspective from which the story is told.

Antecedent Action

Antecedent actions are events that happened before the story begins.

Literary Techniques

Literary techniques activate readers' imaginations. Major events and turning points are often revealed using literary techniques, making the reader invested in the story.

Metaphor

A metaphor is a comparison in which one thing is said to be or have the attributes of something else.

Simile

A simile is a comparison that uses like or as.

Imagery

Imagery is the use of descriptive language to help the reader visualize a scene.

ACTIVITIES

Weblink

Metaphor

Learn more about metaphor in literature by reading the article.

1. How do metaphors allow authors to present unfamiliar ideas? What are the benefits of this? Why do you think Malala chose to use metaphor in the memoir?
2. How are metaphors different from similes and other kinds of analogies? Which of these techniques does Malala employ in the memoir? How effective is their usage? Give examples from the memoir to support your assessment.

More

Examples of Literary Techniques from the Memoir

Analyze the author's use of literary techniques and how they contribute to the narrative of *I Am Malala*.

1. Choose one literary technique used in the memoir. In what particular way did the author use this literary technique? How effective was its usage?
2. What arguments can be made for the use of your chosen literary technique in a text? If this technique were overused or underutilized, what effect might it have on an author's work?

RUBRIC

Analyzing a Video

Students will watch and assess a video related to a component of the memoir, and write an analysis of the video. An exemplary video analysis will meet the following criteria.

- Identifies the purpose of the video
- Identifies the intended audience of the video
- Describes how the content of the video is presented
- Summarizes the information and opinions presented in the video
- Analyzes the quality of the content presented in the video
- Assesses the effectiveness of the video
- Discusses the technical aspects of the video and whether or not these enhance the content
- Determines whether the images and graphics used in the video relate to the content
- Determines whether the video is easy to follow and understand
- Gives the analysis a clear and consistent purpose
- Organizes the analysis in a logical, effective manner
- Presents a strong, clear argument about the video
- Provides strong and accurate details to support the argument about the video
- Considers other perspectives on the purpose and effectiveness of the video
- Makes connections between the video and the memoir
- Properly integrates quotations from the video
- Cites all sources used in the analysis

Theme in the Memoir

Themes are general statements about human nature. In some stories, themes are stated directly, while in others, they are only hinted at and it is up to the reader to interpret them. Authors find different ways to express theme. They might repeat thematic words and phrases, include rhetorical questions, or make allusions to other works of literature or popular culture that share the same theme. In her memoir, Malala makes direct thematic statements about topics that are important to her. She often uses the words and actions of her father to illustrate her themes.

Theme and Purpose

I Am Malala is an extension of Malala's activism. The memoir's purpose is to make the reader aware of the causes for which Malala fights. These are education—especially for girls—and peace.

Education

"I wore one of Benazir Bhutto's white shawls over may favorite pink shalwar kamiz and called on the world's leaders to provide free education to every child in the world. 'Let us pick up our books and our pens,' I said. 'They are our most powerful weapons. One child, one teacher, one book and one pen can change the world.' I didn't know how my speech was received until the audience gave me a standing ovation. My mother was in tears and my father said that had I become everybody's daughter."

Malala Yousafzai, *I Am Malala*, "Epilogue: One Child, One Teacher, One Book, One Pen..."

Major Themes of *I Am Malala*

Malala began life in a **patriarchal** society where the birth of a boy was celebrated, while that of a girl evoked pity. She risked her life to speak out for the right of girls to attend school and witnessed her beloved homeland of Swat ravaged by war. These experiences are the thematic foundations of her memoir. The major themes of *I Am Malala*, in addition to education, are courage, women's rights, and peace.

Courage

"'Are you scared now?' I asked my father.
'At night our fear is strong, Jani,' he told me, 'but in the morning, in the light, we find our courage again.' And this is true for my family. We were scared, but our fear was not as strong as our courage. 'We must rid our valley of the Taliban, and then no one has to feel this fear,' he said."

Malala Yousafzai, *I Am Malala*, "The Clever Class"

Women's Rights

"As in most families, the girls stayed at home while the boys went to school...In the morning when my father was given cream or milk, his sisters were given tea with no milk. If there were eggs, they would only be for the boys. When a chicken was slaughtered for dinner, the girls would get the wings and the neck while the luscious breast meat was enjoyed by my father, his brother and my grandfather. 'From early on I could feel I was different from my sisters,' my father says."

Malala Yousafzai, *I Am Malala*, "My Father the Falcon"

Peace

"My father said only around half the town's population had access to safe drinking water and most, like us, had no sanitation. So he and his friends set up something called the Global Peace Council which, despite its name, had very local concerns. The name was ironic and my father often laughed about it, but the organization's aim was serious: to preserve the environment of Swat and promote peace and education among local people."

Malala Yousafzai, *I Am Malala*, "Children of the Rubbish Mountain"

Secondary Themes

Secondary themes are presented with less emphasis in a story. These themes can add richness and complexity to a story, and give readers a deeper understanding of it. In *I Am Malala*, Malala explores the secondary themes of home, family, culture, altruism, and nature.

ACTIVITIES

Video

The Incomparable Malala Yousafzai

Learn more about Malala's opinions on education by watching this video interview with Ellen DeGeneres.

1. In the interview, Malala recounts her story of finding out that she won the Nobel Peace Prize. Why was it important to her to finish out her school day before talking to the press? How does this reaction reflect the values Malala demonstrates in the memoir?
2. Ellen claims that in America, it is taken for granted that girls go to school, and that they are able to be educated. Why do you think this is the case? Why is it so important to understand that women and children are not treated the same way in other countries? How can spreading awareness contribute to solving this problem?

More

Major and Secondary Themes

Analyze the author's development of themes over the course of the memoir.

1. Choose a secondary theme from this spread and analyze its appearances in the memoir. How does this theme first emerge? Which is the most poignant example of this theme in the memoir?
2. What particular commentary might the author be making about life as a result of this theme's presence in the text? Explain and defend your ideas.
3. Choose a major theme presented on pages 16–17. In what ways does your chosen secondary theme relate to this major theme? Does it deepen or detract from the major theme? How or in what way?

RUBRIC

Creating a Symbolism Poster

Students will choose one of the other symbols listed on page 19 and analyze its role in the memoir. They will then create a poster to present their analysis. An exemplary symbolism poster will meet the following criteria.

- Presents a clear purpose that is conveyed throughout the poster
- Shows an understanding of the concept of symbolism and the role it has in the memoir
- Provides an in-depth analysis of what the symbol represents
- Discusses the role the symbol has in the memoir
- Clearly indicates where the symbol appears in the memoir
- Uses specific, detailed examples from the text to support the analysis
- Makes clear connections to the text
- Properly integrates all quotations
- Organizes the information in a logical, easy-to-read manner
- Includes high-quality graphics that relate to the symbol and effectively enhance understanding of the topic
- Features clear and concise writing
- Uses correct spelling, grammar, and punctuation
- Clearly labels items of importance
- Headings and subheadings are clear and easy to read
- Uses layout to creatively enhances the information
- Creates a poster that is attractive in terms of layout, design, and organization
- Shows a strong effort by the student

Symbolism in the Memoir

Authors often use symbolism to express theme. A symbol can be an object, an action, a word, or an image. Whatever kind of symbol an author chooses, it has meaning apart from its literal definition. Sometimes, authors use symbols that are specific to the story they are writing. In *Moby Dick*, for example, Ahab sees the white whale as a symbol of evil. Authors can also use symbols that are commonly understood. For instance, North American readers typically understand that the dove is a symbol of peace, and that the color white represents innocence. Often, readers must make inferences based on their understanding of an author's work, and of their knowledge of broader literary and cultural traditions, in order to interpret symbols.

Malala's School Bag

Malala's school bag is more than just a holder for her school texts and notebooks. Symbolically, it is a container for her identity as a clever girl, for her ambitions, and for her passionate belief in education. The school bag is a recurring symbol throughout *I Am Malala*. When she describes her shooting in the Prologue, the bag rests at her feet. When education for girls is first threatened, she hides it under her shawl when she walks to school. When war drives the Yousafzais from Swat, she is heartbroken to leave it behind, and overjoyed to find it safe when she returns. When her parents plan to join her in Birmingham, it is the first thing she asks for. Without her school bag—a symbol of her intelligence, desire to learn, and goal to share education with all girls—Malala feels incomplete.

The School Bag

"She also said I must leave my school bag because there was so little room. I was horrified. I went and whispered Quranic verses over the books to try and protect them. Finally everyone was ready. My mother, father, grandmother, my cousin's wife and baby and my brothers all squashed into the back of Dr. Afzal's van along with his wife and children. There were children in the laps of adults and smaller children in their laps. I was luckier—there were fewer people in Safina's car—but I was devastated by the loss of my school bag."

Malala Yousafzai, *I Am Malala*, "Leaving the Valley"

Malala

The School Bag as a Symbol

Awaiting her family's arrival in Birmingham

Returning home after being internally displaced

Going to school after education for girls is forbidden

Other Symbols in the Memoir

Ruined Buddha Statues

As a young girl, Malala played among these stone ruins. The statues were erected when Buddhism was prominent in the Swat region. They symbolize Swat's rich history of peace and tolerance—values that are threatened when the Taliban takes over.

Mountains

Mountains surround Malala's beloved valley. Malala mentions their beauty throughout her memoir. Her best friend, Moniba, associates the mountains and surrounding landscape with peace. For Ziauddin, White Mountain, which rose like a white flag near his home village, also symbolized peace.

Earrings

Earrings have a negative connotation in *I Am Malala*. They are associated with disappointment, dishonesty, and betrayal. Earrings are first mentioned when Malala and her cousins play dress-up and stage a pretend wedding. Earrings adorn the reluctant, crying "bride." Later in the book, Malala, aged seven, steals earrings and other items from her friend. When the Taliban take over Swat, filling the valley with the sound of explosions, a woman is made to regret donating her earrings to their cause.

Burqas

These head-to-toe veils symbolize the oppression of women. This is not a Pashtun tradition, but a foreign practice the Taliban imposes when it comes to Swat. In her memoir, Malala describes how these garments restrict women's vision and movement.

ACTIVITIES

More

What Symbols Appear in the Memoir?

Assess the author's use of symbolism in the memoir.

1. Choose an example from the chart and analyze what the symbol of the school bag represents. For which character is this symbol the most poignant in the memoir? For which character is the symbol least poignant? Argue your opinions with clear reasons.
2. How is this symbol used or reflected in the memoir's themes? Illustrate the ways in which the author's use of language deepens or weakens the meaning of the symbol. Explain and defend your ideas.

Weblink

The Complete Guide to Symbolism

Examine the blog post discussing the usage of symbolism in literature.

1. Contrast and compare examples of analytical descriptions of feelings and sensory descriptions using symbolism from the memoir. Which kind is more effective in the memoir? Provide reasons for your ideas.
2. Should analytical descriptions play a considerable role in the language of a memoir? Why or why not?

The Use of Language

What Is Style?

Authors make choices throughout the process of writing a story. They choose which words to use, how to construct each sentence, and whether to use figurative or literal language. They decide what to write about, whether to adopt a formal or conversational tone, and from whose point of view the story will be told. All of these choices contribute to the author's style. The needs of the reader and the purpose of the text influence the stylistic choices authors make. The purpose of writing might be to persuade, entertain, inform, explain, or describe.

What Is Voice?

The best authors have a distinctive voice that makes their writing recognizable. Malala's voice is plainspoken, but slightly formal—a reminder that English is not her first language. In her writing, the reader sees a balance between her extraordinary intelligence, passion, and courage, as well as the fact that she is, in many ways, a typical young girl.

The Relatable Voice of Malala Yousafzai

"I liked doing my hair in different styles and would spend ages in the bathroom in front of the mirror trying out looks I had seen in movies. Until I was eight or nine my mother used to cut my hair short like my brothers because of lice and also to make it easier to wash and brush as it would get messed up under my shawl. But finally I had persuaded her to let me grow it to my shoulders. Unlike Moniba, who has straight hair, mine is wavy, and I liked to twist it into curls or tie it into plaits. 'What are you doing in there Pisho?' my mother would shout. 'Our guests need the bathroom and everyone is having to wait for you.'"

Malala Yousafzai, *I Am Malala*, "The Clever Class"

Idiom in *I Am Malala*

An idiom is a phrase of figurative language that has become a common saying. Malala's use of idioms adds color to her memoir. Expressions such as "two sides of the same coin" are recognizably English. Others, such as "there cannot be two swords in one sheath," give a taste of Malala's homeland.

Poetry in *I Am Malala*

Malala is proud of her Pashtun heritage. She shares her culture by including some of the poetic language with which she grew up. Malala includes examples of couplets called tapa throughout her memoir, and they appear on the title pages of each of the book's five parts. Toor Pekai's favorite tapa is "Don't kill the doves in the garden./You kill one and the others won't come." Malala remembers her grandmother reciting the tapa "No Pashtun leaves his land of his own sweet will./ Either he leaves from poverty or he leaves for love." Malala's father is a poet, and the book includes verse that he has written: "When the voice of truth rises from the minarets,/The Buddha smiles,/And the broken chain of history reconnects."

Christina Lamb, the co-author of *I Am Malala*, is an **award-winning** journalist and the author of **eight** books.

In addition to **English** and her native **Pashto**, Malala also **speaks Urdu**.

Between **January 3** and **February 19, 2009**, Malala wrote **27 diary entries** for BBC News Urdu.

ACTIVITIES

Document

Contemporary Memoir: A 21st-Century Genre Ideal for Teens

Learn more about the memoir genre by reading this document.

1. Why does *I Am Malala* fall under the genre of memoir? How does Malala use her memoir to "do more than just remember or describe people and events"? Cite textual evidence.
2. It is said in the article that successful contemporary memoirs have a narrative that "permits writers to create meaningful moments that connect to a reader's life experience." Given Malala's unique story, how is it possible for her to accomplish such a connection, particularly with readers from a variety of different backgrounds around the world? Would you say that *I Am Malala* is successful in this respect? Why or why not?

Weblink

Idiom

Find out more about idioms in literature by reading the article.

1. How do Malala's idioms add color to the memoir? Do they fulfill any other functions? Give specific examples from the text to support your answer.
2. In what ways are idioms similar to slang? What are the effects of using such figurative language? How do the use of idioms in *I Am Malala* impact the reader's ability to connect with Malala?

RUBRIC

Writing a Review

Students will write a review of the memoir. An exemplary review will meet the following criteria.

- Grabs the reader's attention with a creative headline
- Begins with an engaging lead to pull the reader into the article
- Introduces the title of the memoir, the author, and the genre
- Provides a brief plot description that does not give away the entire story, and makes the reader want to learn more about the memoir
- Supports arguments about the memoir with accurate and detailed information
- Organizes the review and its arguments in a concise, clear, and logical manner
- Fits the format and style of a review
- Follows the conventions of print or online journalism
- Demonstrates creativity in their approach
- Writes with a unique, engaging voice and perspective
- Provides fresh insight into the memoir
- Provides an honest, authentic opinion on the memoir
- Gives a clear recommendation on the memoir, backed up by specific textual evidence
- Uses correct spelling, grammar, and punctuation

Impact of the Memoir at the Time of Publishing

News of Malala's shooting garnered worldwide attention and gave her a platform to reach powerful decision-makers with her message about the importance of education. On her sixteenth birthday, Malala addressed the United Nations, urging member states to make education a top priority. With *I Am Malala*, she hoped to reach an even wider audience. "I hope the book will reach people around the world," she said, "so they realise how difficult it is for some children to get access to education."

Banned in Pakistan

The memoir received a hostile reception in Pakistan. Critics accused the young author of representing Western interests rather than those of her homeland. The All Pakistan Private Schools Management Association banned the book from the libraries of its 40,000 schools. Another private-school organization banned the book as well, as according to the group's chairman, the memoir was disrespectful to Islam.

Mixed Reviews

I Am Malala was published on October 8, 2013. The book received favorable reviews. Critics writing for *The Washington Post*, the *Los Angeles Review of Books*, and *The Guardian* praised the book for its authentic portrayal of an ordinary teenage girl moved to great courage by extraordinary circumstances. Other reviews, such as those in the *Toronto Star* and *The Globe and Mail*, mixed praise with criticism, stating that the autobiography of such a young protagonist was limited in its ideas and scope.

Honors for Malala

On November 20, 2013, Malala received the Sahkarov Prize for Freedom of Thought. This prize is awarded by the European Parliament to those who dedicate themselves to defending human rights and freedom of expression. In December of that year, she was awarded the United Nations Human Rights Prize, which recognizes outstanding achievements in human rights. The honors continued in 2014. In April of that year, Malala received an honorary doctorate of civil law from the University of King's College in Halifax, Canada. The doctorate recognized her service to education and human rights.

Awards

Despite its mixed reception, Malala's memoir received a number of awards. *I Am Malala* was declared the non-fiction book of the year at the 2013 Specsavers National Book Awards. The audio version of *I Am Malala*, narrated by Neela Vaswani, won the 2015 Grammy for best children's album.

The Nobel Peace Prize

Perhaps the most prestigious honor bestowed on Malala was the Nobel Peace Prize, which she received in October 2014. The Nobel Peace Prize is awarded annually in Oslo, Norway, to honor individuals or organizations who promote peace. Malala shared the award with Kailash Satyarthi, an Indian activist whose organization, Bachpan Bachao Andolan, liberates children from exploitative labor conditions. The Nobel committee recognized Malala and Kailash "for their struggle against the suppression of children and young people and for the right of all children to education." Malala was the youngest person ever to receive the prize.

ACTIVITIES

Document

Book review: 'I Am Malala' by Malala Yousafzai

Analyze the review from *The Washington Post* by Marie Arana, published on October 11,2013.

1. What is the tone of the review? Arana says of the memoir that "[i]t is difficult to imagine a chronicle of a war more moving." Is this a fair assessment? What is it about the way Malala writes that solicits such an emotional response from readers? Give specific examples from the memoir.
2. Arana concludes the review with the claim that Malala is our daughter too, "because she stands for the universal possibility of a little girl." What does this mean? Do you agree with this statement? Explain your answer.

Video

Watch Malala Yousafzai's Nobel Peace Prize acceptance speech

Watch Malala's Nobel acceptance speech from December 10, 2014.

1. In her speech, Malala repeats a couple of key phrases multiple times. Why do you think she does this? What is the effect of this repetition? What are Malala's three goals and how can they be realized?
2. Although she is referred to in many ways by different people, Malala describes herself as "just a committed, and even stubborn person." Is she just being humble, or are her words chosen deliberately, in order to make her more relatable? Explain why you think so. How is the way Malala uses language in her speech similar to the memoir? In what ways does it differ?

RUBRIC

Holding a Classroom Debate

Students will form groups and prepare arguments for a debate on a controversial issue. Exemplary performance in a debate will meet the following criteria.

- Demonstrates in-depth understanding of the topic and related information
- Presents strong, logical, and convincing arguments
- Communicates in a clear and confident manner
- Maintains eye contact
- Uses clear vocal tone and a reasonable rate of vocal delivery
- Uses respectful and appropriate language and body language
- Delivers arguments, evidence, and counter-evidence in an engaging and persuasive manner
- Supports each major point of an argument with several relevant and detailed facts and examples
- Connects all arguments to the overall topic in a clear, concise, and organized manner
- Presents the arguments and supporting evidence in a clear, logical manner
- Presents clear, thorough, and accurate information throughout the debate
- Addresses all of the opposing team's arguments with counter-arguments
- Identifies any weakness in the opposing team's arguments
- Constructs strong and relevant counter-arguments using accurate information
- Presents strong and persuasive arguments throughout the debate
- Summarizes the arguments in the closing statement

Impact of the Memoir Now

Malala's memoir, activism, and awards have brought her global recognition. As a young university student, she tries to balance her role on the international stage with her life as a young woman living away from home for the first time and making new friends. A recognizable figure, Malala continues her campaign and is as outspoken as ever about the right of every child to go to school.

Malala for Young Readers

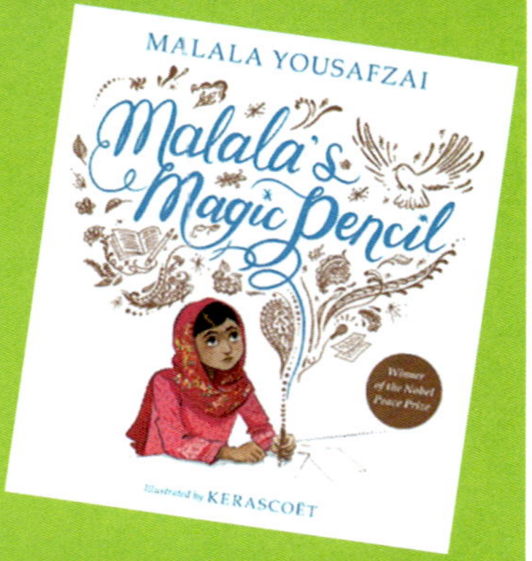

Malala collaborated with author Patricia McCormick to create an edition of her memoir for young readers. This edition leaves out some of the historical and political information of the adult edition. Instead, young readers learn more about Malala's family, particularly her mother and brothers. The young readers edition is appropriate for children in Grades 5 and up. For even younger readers, Malala has written a picture book, *Malala's Magic Pencil*. Like *I Am Malala*, the story is autobiographical. It recounts how a young Malala liked to imagine what she could do with a magic pencil that could both create and erase reality, and how she discovered that she did not need magic, but could make real changes by speaking out.

I Am Malala has sold more than **1.8 million** copies worldwide.

In **2013** and **again in 2015**, Malala was named one of ***Time Magazine's* 100 Most Influential People** in the World.

I Am Malala has been translated into **40 languages**.

Poor No More

The money Malala earned for writing her memoir has enabled the Yousafzai family to leave behind the poverty that characterized their earlier life in Pakistan. Malala reportedly sold the rights to her life story for more than $2 million, and also earns more than $150,000 for each of her speaking engagements. Malala and her parents have established a company called Salarzai Ltd. to manage her income. Unsurprisingly, Malala uses much of her wealth to help others. She and her family have donated more than $1 million to charity.

The Malala Fund

In 2013, Malala and her father founded an organization called the Malala Fund. The aim of the fund is to provide girls around the world with 12 years of education, free of cost and free of danger. The Malala Fund is active in countries where girls' access to education is most limited, such as Pakistan, Afghanistan, India, and Nigeria. It also supports projects in Lebanon, Turkey, and Jordan—countries that host **refugees** from the conflict in Syria that began in 2011.

Returning Home

In March 2018, Malala finally made her dream of returning home a reality. Accompanied by her father and younger brother, Malala visited Pakistan for the first time since the attack on her life, nearly six years prior. While there, she met with Prime Minister Shahid Khaqan Abbasi in Islamabad. Malala also gave an emotional speech, declaring, "Today is the happiest day of my life, because I have returned to my country; I have stepped foot on my nation's soil again and am among my own people." Nonetheless, Malala remains a polarizing figure who continues to face threats from the Taliban.

ACTIVITIES

Video

Malala's Magic Pencil | Malala Yousafzai tells us about her children's book

Learn more about Malala's children's book by watching this video.

1. In the video, Malala says that "wishing wasn't enough. Someone needed to speak out. Why not me?" Why is it important for people to speak out against social injustice? How can Malala's actions inspire others to take action of their own?
2. Malala's hope for the readers of her book is that they "will also realize that they can also find their magic." What does she mean by this? How can finding your magic help to inspire positive change in the world? Give examples to back up your answer.

Document

MALALA's SPEECH

Analyze Malala's address to the United Nations.

1. In her speech, Malala says that "One child, one teacher, one pen and one book can change the world." Is it as simple as Malala claims to start down the path to change? Explain what she means by this assertion.
2. Malala argues that education is the only solution, and demands education first. Do you agree with this position? How effective is education as a tool to combat terrorism? Can you think of any other solutions? Debate this issue citing evidence from the memoir.

RUBRIC

Creating a Timeline

Students will explore a topic related to the memoir and create a timeline to present their research on historical events connected to this topic. An exemplary timeline will meet the following criteria.

- Includes the most significant events pertaining to the topic to be compared and analyzed
- Includes interesting events
- Uses accurate information for all events, including date, location, and major details
- Orders the events in a chronological sequence
- Describes each event with accurate, vivid, and specific details
- Presents the topic from three or more perspectives
- Inspires the reader to ask thoughtful questions regarding the events and perspectives presented in the timeline
- Uses correct spelling, grammar, and punctuation
- Presents the timeline in a visually attractive and striking manner
- Presents the timeline in a neat, organized manner that is logical and easy to follow
- Uses creativity to present the timeline in an engaging manner
- Effectively communicates the historical information relating to the topic
- Supports each event with reliable sources
- Expresses a clear purpose for creating the timeline
- Enhances the reader's understanding of the topic
- Includes a correctly formatted bibliography of all sources used to create the timeline

Perspectives on Terrorism

Terrorism is the use of violence to obtain political or social changes worldwide. Its targets are usually **civilians**. In 2016, terrorist attacks claimed more than 25,000 lives. The attack on Malala was a terrorist attack, since the perpetrators sought to silence her, and to frighten others who fight for women's rights and education into silence as well.

Timeline of Terrorist Attacks Around the World

1985 Air India flight 182 is bombed en route from Toronto to London. Sikh terrorists are responsible for the attack, which kills all 329 people onboard the airplane.

1998 A car bomb is detonated in the town center of Omagh, Northern Ireland, killing 29 people and injuring more than 200 others. The Real Irish Republican Army, a group opposed to peace in the region, claims responsibility for the attack.

1980s

1990s

1995 Extremists Timothy McVeigh and Terry Nichols detonate a truck bomb outside a federal government building in Oklahoma City. The explosion kills 168 people and injures more than 500 others.

2001 Al-Qaeda terrorists hijack and fly airplanes into the World Trade Center in New York City, and the Pentagon in Arlington, Virginia. Almost 3,000 people are killed and 6,000 are injured.

2004 Al-Qaeda-inspired militants board commuter trains in Madrid, Spain, and detonate bombs packed in backpacks and gym bags. The attack kills 191 people and injures more than 1,800.

Malala's fight for education is also a fight for peace and a blow against terrorist attacks such as the one that injured her. Education is one of the most important weapons in the fight against terrorism. It can help to alleviate poverty and **discrimination**, both of which are at the roots of terrorism.

2006 More than 180 people are killed and 800 are injured when bombs are detonated on trains in Mumbai, India. Prosecutors believe that two groups, the Pakistan-based Lashkar-e-Taiba and the Students Islamic Movement of India, are responsible for the attack.

2014 The Nigerian terrorist organization Boko Haram kidnaps 276 girls from their school in Chibok, Nigeria. This sparks the campaign #BringBackOurGirls, which spread around the world and was supported by Malala, First Lady Michelle Obama, and many others.

2011 Norwegian terrorist Anders Breivik kills 77 people in a bombing and a shooting attack. Breivik's targets were the Norwegian government and supporters of multiculturalism and Muslim immigration.

2000s | **2010s**

2008 Gunmen from the Pakistani terror group Lashkar-e-Taiba attack several sites in Mumbai, India, killing 164 people.

2017 An explosives-laden truck explodes in Mogadishu, Somalia, killing more than 300 people. The terrorist group al-Shabab is presumed responsible for the attack.

2014 Taliban terrorists attack a school in Peshawar, Pakistan. 141 people are killed, including 132 children.

ACTIVITIES

Transparency–Timeline

Timeline of Terrorist Attacks Around the World

Examine the historical and cultural contexts shown on the timeline. Then, contrast and correlate its elements with the themes and events presented in *I Am Malala*.

1. In what ways can historical events, culture, and social mores influence a population's perspective on terrorism? How might these elements have shaped the way a reader in the early 2010s interpreted the memoir?
2. How might the era in which Malala Yousafzai wrote *I Am Malala* have influenced the memoir's themes and settings? Where in the memoir is this most evident? Explain your reasoning.
3. Which current events, changes in laws, new ideas, or political discussions are terrorism in the world today? Which ideas and attitudes are still prevailing? Why?
4. How might current events and present perspectives affect the way a reader interprets the memoir? Why is it important for readers to understand the era and context in which a memoir is written?

RUBRIC

Writing a Comparative Essay

Students will compare two literary devices used in the memoir, and then write a comparative essay based on their analysis. An exemplary comparative essay will meet the following criteria.

- Consists of a one-paragraph introduction, three body paragraphs, and a one-paragraph conclusion
- Introduction includes an engaging lead statement about the topic of the essay, more detailed information about the memoir, and a one-sentence thesis that specifically states the essay's argument
- Body paragraphs include a topic sentence that refers to the thesis and how the idea appears in the memoir, a supporting sentence that points to this part of the memoir, textual evidence of this idea from the memoir, and analysis of this evidence
- Body paragraphs end with a transition to the next paragraph
- Conclusion refers to the topic of the essay and the three points presented in the body paragraphs, and restates the thesis
- Provides a thorough analysis of the literary devices in question
- Cites strong and thorough textual evidence to support analysis of what the memoir says explicitly
- Presents a clear, specific thesis that indicates a high level of critical engagement
- Organizes ideas in a logical manner
- Communicates arguments in a clear, effective manner
- Properly integrates all quotations
- Correctly cites all sources used
- Correctly formats bibliography

Writing a Comparative Essay

I Am Malala is a portrait of courage, a love letter to Swat, and a call to action. Malala tells her story with engaging character sketches, vivid descriptions, and thought-provoking themes. After studying the memoir, write a comparative essay to explore how two literary devices are used in *I Am Malala*. This could be a comparison of characters, themes, symbols, or settings. To write a comparative essay, you will need to formulate an argument. Your argument should clearly state how your compared elements are similar or different. Support your argument with sufficient evidence from the memoir and valid reasoning.

How to Analyze and Compare Characters

Use the chart to guide your comparison of two characters in *I Am Malala*.

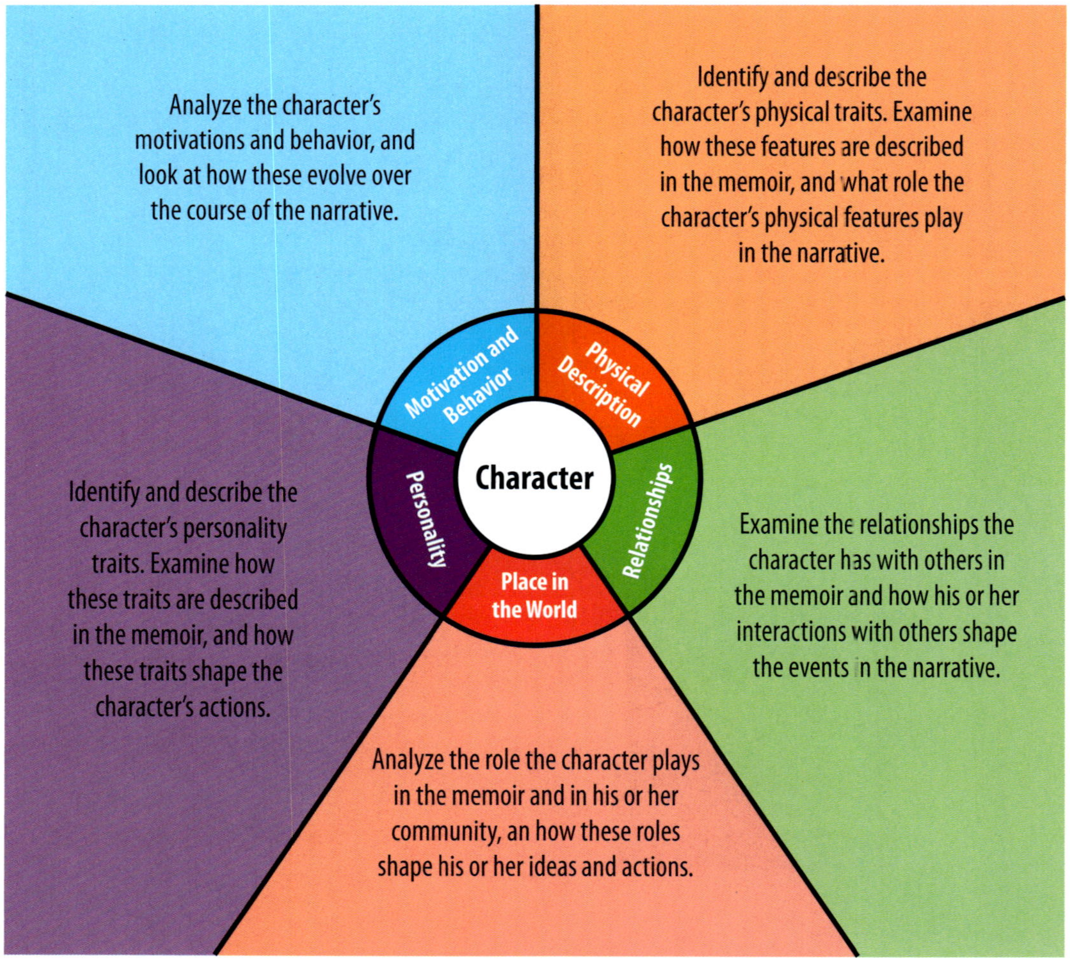

Comparing Malala with Moniba

Malala

Physical Description
- Petite
- Has her father's dark skin, wide nose, and brown eyes

Personality
- Brave
- Intelligent
- Competitive
- Altruistic
- Outspoken
- Forgiving

Motivation and Behavior
- Passionate about education and women's rights
- Wants to please her parents
- Loves her homeland
- Desires peace

Relationships
- Is her parents' firstborn child and only daughter
- Has two younger brothers, with whom she quarrels
- Is best friends with Moniba
- Has a rival for top marks at school—Malka-e-Noor

Place in the World
- Was raised without the limitations her culture usually places on girls
- Became a well-known activist in Pakistan and later, around the world
- Is famous around the world following her shooting
- Has met world leaders, addressed international organizations, and won prestigious awards

Moniba

Place in the World
- A good student with strong speaking and writing skills
- Lost family members to a suicide bomber
- Must defer to her brothers, whom she fears could make her leave school

Motivation and Behavior
- Guards her reputation
- Enjoys the *Twilight* book series and Bollywood television shows
- Speaks out for the right of girls to attend school
- Says she wants to be a doctor, but really wants to be a fashion designer

Physical Description
- Beautiful
- Pale skin
- Straight hair

Relationships
- Has three sisters and four brothers
- Is like a big sister to Malala
- Is Malala's best friend and confidante
- Makes the rules in her friendship with Malala

Personality
- Wise
- Possessive and jealous at times
- Competitive
- Hardworking
- Intelligent
- Peace-loving
- Flirtatious

ACTIVITIES

More

Questions for Character Analysis

Analyze how specific character features, such as conflicts, motivations, relationships, place in the world, and personality affect the plot of *I Am Malala*. Cite strong and thorough textual evidence to support your analysis of what the memoir says explicitly as well as the inferences you may have drawn from the memoir's setting, themes, and symbols.

Quiz Answers

1. A
2. C
3. A
4. C
5. D
6. B
7. D
8. C
9. C
10. B

Key Words

activist: someone who tries to bring about social change through vigorous campaigning

advocate: supporting or speaking in favor of a cause

assassination: the murder of a public figure for political motives

civilians: people who are not members of a military or police force

code of conduct: a set of rules describing the attitudes and behaviors expected of a particular group

democracy: a system of government in which the will of the people is enacted by elected representatives

discrimination: unfair treatment based on prejudice

drone: an aircraft or missile operated by remote control

extremism: fanatical political or religious opinions

imam: someone who leads prayers in a mosque

Industrial Revolution: major economic change marked by the introduction of power-driven machinery

internally displaced persons: people forced to flee their homes and seek safety elsewhere within their own country

militants: aggressive or violent activists

patriarchal: a society in which men dominate and are considered superior to women

refugees: people forced to leave their own country to escape war, persecution, or disaster

Taliban: a fundamentalist Islamic movement that gained influence in Afghanistan and Pakistan in the 1990s and early 2000s

terrorists: people who use violence and intimidation to bring about political or social change

Literary Terms

antecedent action: background events that take place before the first event in the plotline of a narrative

conflict: a struggle between two or more opposing forces, creating a tension that must be resolved

flashback: the narration of events that happened before the present moment in a story

flash-forward: the narration of events that happen after the present moment in a story

idiom: a commonly used word or phrase that has a figurative meaning

imagery: the use of language to create a picture in the mind of the reader or listener

metaphor: a comparison in which one thing is said to be, or have the characteristics of, something else

narrative: a logically arranged series of events presented for an audience; a story

non-fiction: literature that recounts events that actually happened

plot: the specific action that propels a story forward

point of view: the perspective from which a story is narrated

simile: a comparison that uses "like" or "as"

style: the unique way in which writers use language to tell their story; this can include word choice, the use of imagery, and the length and organization of sentences

symbolism: a stylistic device using symbols to represent and intensify concepts and ideas

theme: the underlying topic, idea, or position in a work that is often a general, universal statement about life

voice: a writer's distinct personality and form of expression, as shown through his or her written work

Index

Published by Smartbook Media Inc.
350 5th Avenue, 59th Floor New York, NY 10118
Website: www.openlightbox.com

Library of Congress Cataloging-in-Publication Data
Names: Lomberg, Michelle, author. | Gillespie, Katie, author.
Title: I am Malala / Michelle Lomberg and Katie Gillespie.
Description: New York, NY : Smartbook Media, Inc., [2019] | Series: Lightbox literature studies | Includes index.
Identifiers: LCCN 2018000593 (print) | LCCN 2018001899 (ebook) | ISBN 9781510537132 (Multi-User eBook) | ISBN 9781510537125 (hard cover : alk. paper)
Subjects: LCSH: Yousafzai, Malala, 1997- | Young women--Education--Pakistan--Biography. | Children's rights--Pakistan. | Women social reformers--Pakistan--Biography. | Literature--Study and teaching--Activity programs.
Classification: LCC LC2330 (ebook) | LCC LC2330 .Y68 2019 (print) | DDC 371.822095491--dc23
LC record available at https://lccn.loc.gov/2018000593

Printed in Brainerd, Minnesota, United States
1 2 3 4 5 6 7 8 9 0 22 21 20 19 18

062018
121017

Editor: Katie Gillespie
Art Director: Terry Paulhus

The publisher acknowledges Getty Images, iStock, Alamy, and Wikimedia Commons as its primary image suppliers for this title.